The

Instant Guide to

Project Management

by *Chris Croft*

Contents

Chapter		Page
1	Define the project	2
2	List the tasks	7
3	Estimate times and costs	10
4	Find the critical path	13
5	Consider crashing tasks	16
6	Draw Gantt chart	17
7	Resource requirements	20
8	Assess risks	25
9	Monitor progress	28
10	Monitor cumulative cost	30
11	Readjust your plan	33
12	Review: learn and praise	39

1. Define the Project

This is the most important part of the project! Getting this wrong and you will be doomed to a nightmare project – months of pain and suffering! Take some time to make sure you know what you are trying to do before you wade in.

- Agree the success criteria and major constraints with the customer, in writing.

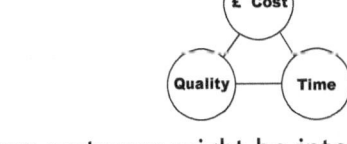

- Your customer might be internal or external, might be your boss, or you may have a number of customers (stakeholders). You need to know what they ALL want.

- Success criteria will be in terms of Time taken, Cost (which will partly be from hours worked), and Quality (what they get, exactly).

- Quality should have a measurable acceptance test.
- List anything that the project depends on – funding, decisions, resources from the customer or from within the organisation.
- There should probably be a kick-off meeting, where the Project Manager (PM), the customer/client, and if necessary Sales / Commercial all discuss and agree the above details.
- At this meeting, or earlier, probe your customer for key drivers – are the time cost and quality MUST-haves or just nice-to-haves. Do this by asking why that date/budget, what if we went late/over, and see if they are interested in trading for example more time for a higher specification. Knowing the key driver will be extremely useful when/if the project gets into difficulties later.
- Consider negotiating some contingency into the time, cost and specification at this stage.
- Negotiation means if possible getting the client to open – they should tell you how

much they can afford, when they need completion, and the ideal specification they would have.

- Negotiation also means knowing your walk-away point in advance. This is the point (or points in terms of combinations of time quality and money) at which you feel that the project cannot be done and at which you will say "You'll have to get someone else if you are going to insist on this specification – because I can't do it and I don't want to make promises I can't keep".

- Be assertive – don't be pushed into agreeing anything that you feel is impossible (or unlikely) to achieve just because that's an easy option or you want the client to be happy. In the end everyone will be less happy if you do this – including you!

- In order that the PM can have a strong case to argue, and in order to have a plan to agree and sign off, it will be necessary to have done some planning before this kick-off meeting. Therefore steps 2-8 in this book will need to be done, at least in brief, before step 1. They may have to be re-visited after step 1 is complete.

- PMYS: Planning Makes You Stronger!

- There should be a specification document or Project Initiation Document which is **signed** by the project manager to say that they are happy and can achieve the task, and **by the client** to say that they will be happy with what has been promised. This protects both the customer (from under-delivery) and the Project Manager (from the client adding extra requirements, moving the goal posts, and complaining afterwards that it wasn't exactly what they wanted).

- This 'PID' should contain evidence like lists of tasks, cost estimates, and a gantt chart, but this is not extra work because you'll have to do these anyway in order to know whether the project is possible and then in order to carry it out.

- The PID should also contain an assessment of risks, in order to show the client that you are aware of these, and that you are working to minimise them, but also so that the client can sign to say that they are prepared to live with this level of risk.

- Successful completion of the project will require a suitable team – both quantity and quality. Team members could be formally invited and signed up, with an estimate of how many days / weeks will be required – and if they have a different line manager, he or she may need to sign up to letting them go for the full required time.

2. List the tasks

- Involve the team
- Brainstorm a list of all of the tasks that might be involved in the project
- Put the tasks in some sort of logical diagram – often known as a Work Breakdown Structure

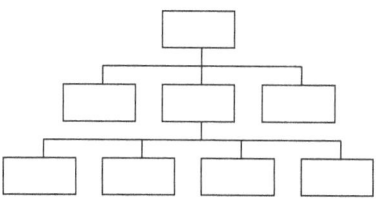

- Remember equalities: are there any issues affecting others that you might have forgotten at this stage?
- Consider "granularity" – how detailed should the task breakdown be?

- If you don't go granular enough you'll have difficulty fitting tasks into the network diagram later; you'll find yourself wanting to say "ongoing", which is not allowed. But remember, "It's Never Too Late To Granulate" so you just chop them up a bit more later.

- If you have more than about 10 tasks then it's probably going to be better to have some sub-projects, where you break those tasks down into more detail on a separate page

- Remember that managing the project is a task in itself, and should have time allowed for it

- Have a look at previous project WBSs for ideas

- Have a look at previous project reviews to see what others have missed

- Show your WBS to an expert, or someone who has done a similar project before – and ask them what you have forgotten
- Remember that any tasks forgotten at this stage will make your project go both late and over budget!

3. Estimate times and costs for each task

- Base your estimates on experience, records of previous projects, and your team's judgments
- Allow for optimists and pessimists in your team – apply your own judgment
- Estimate the maximum it might take/cost - and the minimum
- Don't promise the average to your customer – you will have a 50% failure rate!

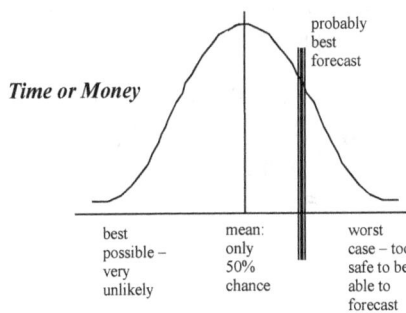

- Add up the averages and then add in some contingency
- Get contingency in time, cost, and perhaps even specification
- If necessary spread the contingency in small amounts across all of the tasks so that it is not easily seen or removed
- Putting in contingency is not dishonest – it is part of the genuine estimating process. The time taken, and the cost, will be the sum of all the known tasks plus some unknown ones, and we must allow for these if we are going to avoid letting the customer down. We are doing it for THEM!
- The objective of putting in some contingency is to be able to give the customer an estimate that is reliable – or at least 90% reliable.

- There are many ways for your project to take longer or cost more than you thought, but not many ways for it to be better. If there was a better way then that would already be your plan!

- It is probably not a good idea to tell the customer about the contingency. Keeping it from them is not dishonest! They don't really want to know about it, and it will only worry them if they know that there is risk involved and that they are paying for this. If asked, just admit to a little: "I've put in a few days to cover the unexpected".

4. Find the critical path

Consider dependencies and draw the CPA network: and find the float of the non-critical tasks

- Don't try to do this in your head
- Customers will either expect to see it, or be impressed by it
- Activity on node (tasks in boxes with times on the boxes, often called CPM) is probably a better way to draw the network...

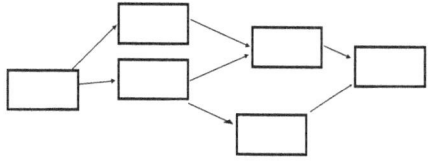

...than activity on arrow (aka PERT) where the tasks and times go on the arrows and the arrows point to circular "events":

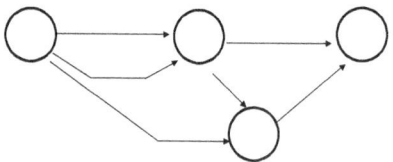

- This is because CPM shows the actual work to be done, and often there are no significant events between activities.
- You can add milestones or events to your CPM diagram if you wish
- The critical path is the longest route through the diagram, and is the quickest you can do the entire project
- Draw it neatly - if you have arrows crossing over there is an increased risk of missing the critical path
- Tasks on the critical path need careful estimating, since they define the lead time of the project, and later they will need careful monitoring if the project is to remain on schedule

- Non-critical tasks have float – you can choose whether to start them straight away or whether to do them later. Doing them straight away is safer, but doing them later may delay expenditure, and my enable you to have more information by the time you do the task. Considerations of float are best done using the Gantt chart – see later.

5. Consider crashing or overlapping critical tasks

- If the critical path is too long you may decide to overlap tasks – this is usually more risky, but quicker.
- Your other choice is to crash a task – which means throw money (or people) at it in order to do it more quickly. This usually means it will be more expensive in the end, and possibly of a lower quality too.
- If you crash a critical task there is a risk that something else in parallel with it will become critical as well.
- The best tasks to crash are those which are a) critical, b) long, and c) not in parallel with others.

6. Draw Gantt (bar) chart

Gantt charts have three main purposes:

- Communication: to show everyone when their tasks will be started and finished
- Loading: to be able to look vertically at any given week or month and consider whether you have the resources for all the tasks being done at that time
- Monitoring Progress: by colouring in the Gantt chart and trying to keep up with the "Today" line (see step 9, on page 23).

- The Gantt chart may be on a computer, either Microsoft Project or just an Excel spreadsheet, or it may be on paper, or on a whiteboard on the wall
- Draw in the critical path first, then put the floating tasks (see A & B) around it

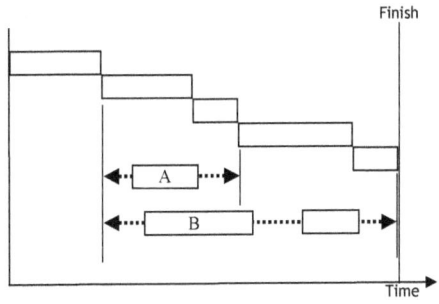

- Adjust the floating tasks in order to level out the load profile (e.g. move B to the right)
- Then issue the Gantt chart for everyone to see the plan and to see how they fit in.

7. Calculate resource requirements over time

You can adjust the load each week/month using float of non-critical tasks

- You may be planning the resource loading (people or hours required) for just one large project, or perhaps a collection of small projects
- An excel spreadsheet can be a good way to do this, using trial and error and looking at the column totals, or you may prefer to move pieces of cardboard around on a square grid
- The columns in your spreadsheet may be in hours worked per week per person, or days per week, or fractions of a person employed in each week.

- If your project is time limited the question is "without breaking the critical path, what's the smoothest profile we can get by moving the floating tasks around, and how high does the profile go?"

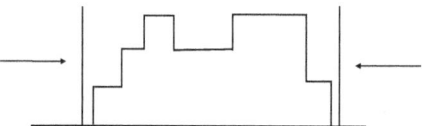

- If your project is resource limited the question is "How long will it take us with the limited number of people that we have?".

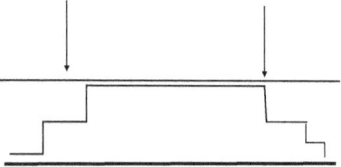

- In order to cope with limited resources you may have to break the critical path and take longer. Note that this creates a new critical path, so different jobs will require careful monitoring during the carrying out of the project.
- Tricks for time limited projects are to crash or overlap tasks – these tend to have a cost in terms of money and/or quality
- Tricks for resource limited projects are breaking a task and finishing it later, and stretching a task (doing it with half a person taking twice as long) which also tend to have a cost in terms of money and/or quality
- If a project is both time- and resource-limited then the quality will probably have to be reduced – not ideal!

- A loading plan is well worth having, even though the reality will be different – people will join and leave the project, be ill, etc. But you still need a plan to be able to roughly plan, and without a plan you could start a project with a promised progress rate that is going to be impossible to achieve.
- The plan needs to include holidays booked by team members.
- Your load plan will give you a logical base from which to argue against interferences like people being taken off your project, or other work being pushed in as a higher priority. These are OK as long as the clearly-visible resulting effects on your project are agreed with all.

- If you have a number of projects running at once you could have one big MOAG (Mother Of All Gantts) showing everything. This will help you plan (and make you stronger), for example if a new project is added then either you will need more people or other projects will have to slip.

8. Assess risks, and prepare action plans

- Brainstorm a list of everything that could go wrong with your project.
- Use your team and the reviews from other projects to get the longest list possible.
- For each possible problem, assess how likely it is to happen and how serious it would be. Multiplying a rating for each allows you to prioritise the risks, or have a cut-off point below which you ignore them.
- For each possible problem, find ways to make it less likely to happen (by tackling the cause or causes). These preventative actions should be built into your project plan.
- For each possible problem, find ways to make it less serious if it does happen. This involves having back-up plans ready. You need to cover all of the possible effects of the problem which may occur.

- Only show your customer the external risk plan – they don't need to know about potential internal problems.
- Make sure there's enough contingency in terms of time and money to cover the likely risks.
- Remember that the purpose of contingency is not to make life easy for you, but to ensure that the project comes in on time and to budget – in other words, to make the customer happy.

This is the end of the planning phase. All of the above actions need to be done before you agree to take the project on.

The actions that follow are for the implementation part of the project.

9. Monitor progress to the Gantt chart

- Colour in the tasks when they are complete (for some tasks you may decide to colour in a proportion that is completed, but there is a risk of optimism here)
- Keep up with the "today" line

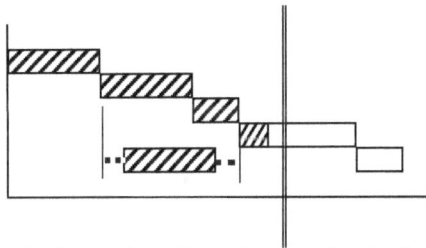

- Watch the critical tasks particularly closely – they are the ones that define whether the project goes late or not.
- If the project has gone irretrievably late you may decide to slip the whole Gantt chart and reissue a new, slipped, one (see step 11, on page 27)

- Ideally the Gantt chart would be displayed on a wall for all to see so that there is pressure on everyone to do their promised bit.

- If you are managing a project manager the one question you need to ask every now and then is "Can I see your coloured in Gantt chart?"

10. Monitor cumulative cost

- You may get figures on spend to date from Accounts. These may or may not be out of date, inaccurate, and/or categorized into sections that are not helpful.
- If you don't get figures, or they are not suitable, you will need to keep your own records of your expenditure – perhaps on a spreadsheet.
- Remember that comparing actual expenditure to date against planned expenditure to date is MEANINGLESS!! If you are underspent it could be because you really are spending less than planned, or because you are running late.

- Comparing the spend status with your coloured-in Gantt chart showing progress will give you the full picture:

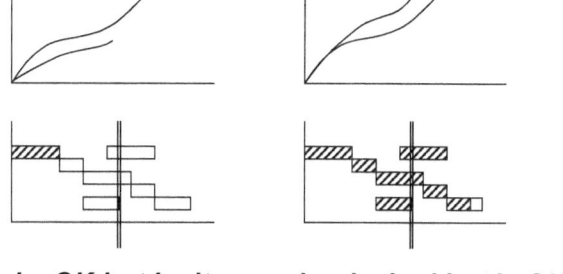

Looks OK but isn't   **Looks bad but is OK**

- Beware of 'late + overspent' looking OK financially. This is the commonest, worst, hardest to spot, and hardest to recover.

- Useful measures are

Schedule Performance Index
(are we keeping up?)

and

Cost Performance Index
(are we spending more than we should, per task?).

- You should also have estimates of expected completion date and forecast cost at completion.
- If you are managing a number of project managers you could ask for these each month. Then you can keep an eye on all of the projects at a glance, and also watch for slippage on the forecasts which you receive each month.

11. Readjust your plan

Monitor progress by holding a weekly or monthly review meeting. Use a Gantt chart to assess lateness.

If the project is running late you have only 4 options:

1. Crash the project by spending more money (e.g. overtime, outside contractors etc) on some of the critical tasks
2. Crash the project by reducing the quality of some of the critical tasks
3. Crash the project by overlapping some of the critical tasks
4. Let the project slip
5. Do nothing and hope that it fixes itself.

Clearly if time is the main consideration then you have to choose option 1, if it's cost then option 2, if it's quality then option 4. Option 3 could save you time without costing money or quality, but usually adds risk and is not always possible at all. Option 5 is the most tempting but is ALWAYS a bad idea!

Whatever you choose to do, you must tell everyone as soon as possible. This means customer/stakeholders/sponsors, and also your team.

You may be able to negotiate some extra money if some or all of the problems have come from the customer moving goal posts.

At this stage you'll be glad you
 a) wrote a PID and
 b) kept some contingency.

Above all, avoid...

the Three Crimes of Rescheduling:

- Too early
- Too late
- Twice

This means rescheduling only in the middle third of the project, putting in extra contingency when you reschedule, and then keeping a very close watch on it after that.

You will need to be seen to be leading the project. This means:

- Regular progress meetings with your team
- Meetings with the customer as well as with the team – keep them informed of problems sooner rather than later
- Delegation of tasks and of the sorting out of problems
- Motivation – encouragement, conveying the importance of the task
- Thanks and appreciation
- Supporting / coaching individuals.
- Remaining positive in the face of adversity
- Encouraging the team to be honest – don't shoot the messenger

- Management by wandering about:

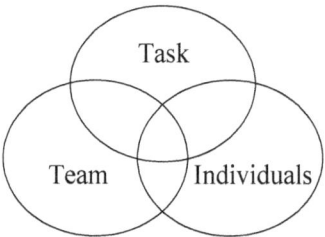

> are tasks progressing as planned and as reported?
> is the team working well together?
> are individuals happy and motivated?
> what might go wrong?

- Doing some of the tasks in order to show willing and to show competence, while not being drawn in and losing the overview
- For tasks where progress is hard to monitor (e.g. team member writing software) keep tabs on their estimated completion date – is it slipping?
- You may find it useful to keep a diary, perhaps weekly, just in note form, where you record current problems, planned solutions, did they work, expected completion date. Reading this back at the end of the project could be a very useful learning experience.

12. Review: learn and praise

- The only time you, the team, and the organisation can learn
- Meet as a group, with a flip-chart
- Project Manager does not do the writing, but sits in the group
- What was good, that we would want to repeat and to tell others to do in similar projects?
- What was not so good, that we could advise others to avoid
- What could we have done even better, knowing what we now know?
- Document the above and keep all the reviews in one place – on the intranet, or in a file where each project has just one side of A4 for its review

- Requires a no-blame culture and honest "owning up"
- Requires finding the time (and maybe a number to book it to) even for projects which are overspent – in fact especially for those!
- Categories which might be useful to consider during the review: were sufficient resources available? was the customer happy or not (and why?), quality of the original proposal / initiation document, contractor relations and performance, and any opportunities for future work.
- You might also review the performance of team members with them and/or with their line manager – significant achievements, areas of strength, and areas for development.

- The review is an opportunity to thank the team, perhaps even celebrate completion of the project – maybe you could all go and have a pizza or a curry?

This book was produced by

Chris Croft

Chris runs training courses on
- Project Management
- Time Management
- Leadership
- Negotiation
- and other subjects

he can be contacted on

01202-747480
34 Parkstone Heights
Poole   BH14 0QF

www.chriscrofttraining.co.uk
chris@chriscrofttraining.co.uk

Chris Croft Training

www.ingramcontent.com/pod-product-compliance
Lightning Source LLC
Chambersburg PA
CBHW070433180526
45158CB00017B/1169